ACTOR/AUTHOR
Clive Francis as the repugnant Mr Hough

A Small Family Business, the National Theatre, 1987

Laugh Lines

Caricatures by Clive Francis

Foreword by John Gielgud

HODDER AND STOUGHTON
London   Sydney   Auckland   Toronto

British Library Cataloguing in Publication Data
Francis, Clive
  Laugh lines: caricatures.
  1. English caricatures. Special subjects. Actors &
  actresses
  I. Title
  741.5'942

ISBN 0-340-49601-0

Published by Hodder and Stoughton,
a division of Hodder and Stoughton Ltd,
Mill Road, Dunton Green, Sevenoaks, Kent TN13 2YA
Editorial Office: 47 Bedford Square, London WC1B 3DP

Designed by Trevor Spooner from a concept by Clive Francis

Printed in Great Britain by Butler and Tanner Ltd,
Frome and London

FOR NATALIE

WITH LOVE

Acknowledgments

I'm greatly indebted to everyone concerned for the time and care taken in contributing captions to their caricatures – as opposed to suing me in the High Courts!

My thanks, also, to Sir John Gielgud, for his delightful foreword and for allowing me to use an extract from his autobiography *An Actor and his Time* (Sidgwick & Jackson). Lord Olivier for allowing me to quote freely from his *Confessions of an Actor* and *On Acting* (both Weidenfeld & Nicolson).

My thanks also to my photographer Roy Cook, my agent David Watson, and Stephen Wood and his hard-working team at the National. And to Mobil who so generously sponsored my 1988 exhibition at the National Theatre, from which this book was a direct result; and to my dear family and friends for all their loyal and loving support.

Clive Francis

Anthony Quayle, Dandy Dick, 1986

CONTENTS

Tommy Steele, 1983

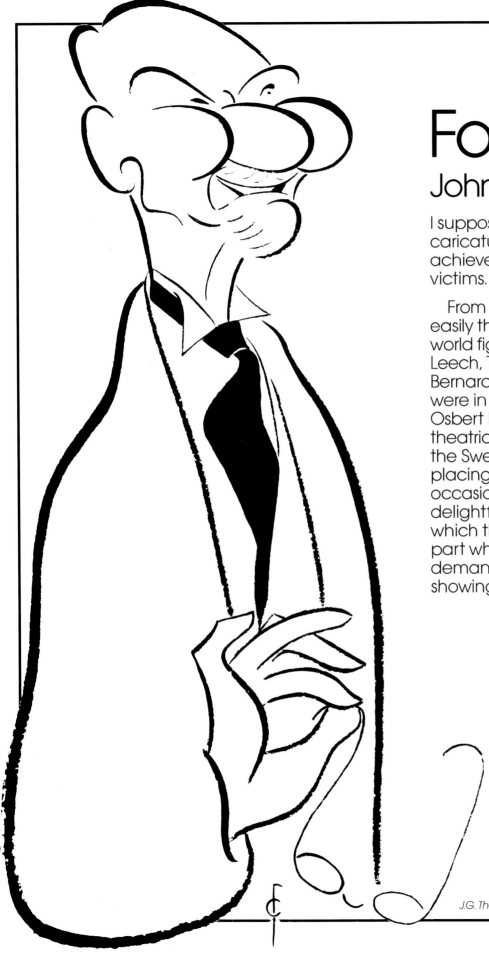

Foreword
John Gielgud

I suppose that the first task facing a successful caricaturist is, like that of the photographer, to achieve an instantly recognisable likeness of his victims.

From my boyhood I was brought up to recognise easily the somewhat sedate images of Royalty and world figures in the cartoons of *Punch*, drawn by Leech, Tenniel and Sambourne, Raven Hill and Bernard Partridge (Max Beerbohm's wispy celebrities were in a different class). I greatly admired Low and Osbert Lancaster, as I grew older, and, in the theatrical scene, Haselden, Tom Titt, and especially the Swedish artist, Nerman, with his decorative placing and use of black and white, with occasional touches of red. His work has found a delightful successor in the work of Clive Francis which this book supplies. To caricature a player in a part which necessitates some sort of disguise must demand a particular kind of observation in showing both the stage character and the individual personality creating it.

Cartoons are, of course, a somewhat different proposition from caricatures, though they must so frequently include them. But, in the world of such swift changes, their political comment may often be so

J.G. The Best of Friends, Apollo Theatre, 1988

highly topical that in a few years they may become out-dated and even difficult to understand. The even more ephemeral world of the theatre requires similar demands in immediate effectiveness, as plays come and go and can be so quickly forgotten.

Though at first it may be flattering to find one has been singled out by caricaturists – even in the grotesque fantasies of 'Spitting Image', it is scarcely possible not to be somewhat appalled by the necessary blow to one's own personal vanity. But Clive Francis has a more benign approach to his subjects than the merciless artists, Scarfe, for instance, or Topolski – whose brilliant, but often revolting caricatures are, to my mind, only justified by their prodigious talents – and I congratulate him most warmly on this selection of his work, which he has so diligently and delightfully pursued in addition to his distinguished stage career.

John Gielgud

Introduction

Where the interest and fascination for caricature came from I've never understood, except through my love of the theatre and my early idolatry of theatre people (which after twenty-five years in the profession, has never left me).

As a dotty young fan I used to spend my Saturday afternoons crouched at the stage-door of Eastbourne's Devonshire Park Theatre shyly asking for autographs from the top West-End actors of the day. A. E. Matthews once emerged after a performance of *The Chiltern Hundreds* and seeing me proffer my dog-eared programme threw his arms around me and said, 'Ah, Gladys, thank God you came round.' He was, I hasten to add, extremely old and *very* short-sighted.

When I was in my early teens I began attending Saturday morning classes at the local art school. A Miss Glover was in attendance. A stout middle-aged lady with grey hair parted in the centre and then circuitously plaited around each side of her head. I took great exception to being told how to draw my tree or paint my cloud, and felt an arrogant need to express myself freely and individually regardless of form and perspective – actually it was just pure laziness on my part, finding no interest in Miss Glover's still-life arrangements or daubing large sheets of (what seemed like) rice paper, with a lot of poster paint.

So at the tender age of thirteen I gave up my art education and simply relied on instinct – a painfully slow and unbalanced approach, which is still proving, through my lack of life class attendances, tedious and frustrating.

My great-uncle, Donald Towner, was a truly superb and highly acclaimed artist in both water-colours and oils, and was as familiar to the residents of Hampstead (where he lived in great Georgian splendour) as he was to every square inch of the South Downs, where he could be seen tramping (God-like, his snow white hair and beard billowing before him) in search of new locations. Whenever an excursion to London was planned, and if my uncle happened to be free, a trip around the National or Tate galleries would invariably take place.

This was an event I always looked forward to, because, apart from being an interesting and amusing companion, he was also a great teacher and had the ability to stimulate the senses, train the eye and impart knowledge in an absorbing and intriguing way. It was through him that I discovered the sumptuous flamboyancy of Beardsley, finding the exotic style of his graphic design greatly influential. As I did with the posters of Toulouse-Lautrec, with his sharply defined caricatures of the Parisian music hall – Yvette Guilbert with that gorgeous smudge of lipstick. Then later on, as I became more and more interested and caught up in the subject, my influences shifted as well, from Max

Beerbohm's dandified impressions through to those of Oscar Berger, Nicolas Bentley, Nerman (with his tantalising usage of red), Sherriffs, Levine, Ronald Searle and the great Al Hirshfeld. Every one of which has helped me over the years to re-think and re-shape my ideas of imagery.

But it was to the stage and becoming an actor that my heart was first set. And so in 1961 I joined the Penguin Players weekly repertory, Bexhill-on-Sea, prior to going to the R.A.D.A., and entering what has turned out to be an extremely happy and fulfilling career in the theatre.

I have been fortunate in that most of my caricatured victims have either been colleagues that I've worked with, at one time or another, or know well on a purely personal level. So that I have been able, for example, to observe at close hand through rehearsal an actor grow and gradually transform himself into his or her character. The backs of my scripts have been, in a sense, my artistic notebooks, full of short-hand squiggles and blobs representing nostrils shaped like tadpoles, eyes twirling themselves into lengths of liquorice and mouths twisted into gaping pot-holes.

It was while rehearsing a television adaptation of *Caesar and Cleopatra* that Alec Guinness spotted me crouched in some dingy corner of the drill-hall scribbling away furiously. When he enquired what I was 'adoing', and discovered that I was in fact lampooning – for my own amusement – other members of the cast, he looked at me suspiciously and graciously declined to view the likeness that I had done of him. So that it was deeply gratifying when fourteen years later I was asked, at his request, to design the book jacket for his autobiography *Blessings in Disguise.*

And then there was the occasion when I was rehearsing for Laurence Olivier's television production of *Saturday, Sunday, Monday.* A few days before we went into the studio, somebody discovered that 'Sir's' birthday was imminent – his seventieth, in fact – and that something suitable ought to be found to mark the event. I suggested, somewhat naïvely, never expecting to be taken seriously, that I drew a little cameo of him in character as the hat-destroying old grandfather, Antonio, and that the cast had it neatly framed. Well, the onus of responsibility that I felt as to how this birthday gift would be received, made me extremely nervous – verging on paranoia. And when after three days there was still no word as to his reaction, I suspected the worst and decided to ask him outright what he thought of his little 'prezzie'. 'Darling boy, I thought it was charmingly witty and so clever, so *very* clever. It will hang – no offence, dear boy, *believe me* – in my lavatory, a very special spot in my household.' Ten years later the National Theatre celebrated his eightieth birthday with an all-star gala, and asked me to design the cover of the souvenir programme – the original of which now hangs in mine.

Not every actor has relished the way I've brush-stroked their features into objects of general derision. Rex Harrison reacted simply with, 'You Bugger'. Caricature in a way is rather akin to plastic surgery. As bits are taken away so bits are added on. The only difference being that the caricaturist reveals, unmercilessly, warts, tucks and all.

Someone once described my drawings as bold and sympathetic. Bold, I can hopefully understand, because that signifies an economic flow of line which is what I strive for with each and every design – not always easily accomplished, simplicity being by far the most complex equation to unravel. But sympathetic! That seems to evoke a note of compassion, a degree of sympathy towards the subject as though I felt sorry for them for looking the way they do. Which is certainly *not* the case!

No, in all seriousness, I would define my work as tongue in cheek portraiture – so long as the right tongue is 'sympathetically' well embedded in the right cheek!

Clive Francis

IN MEMORY OF MY FATHER RAYMOND,
a wonderful and enchanting actor
who viewed life with a generous pinch of salt.
Or, in his case – snuff!

I try to change my height.
To shrink towards the end of the play. I dunno why.
It just seems to me to be right.
Giving in. Being subservient at the end.

MICHAEL GAMBON

A View from the Bridge, the National Theatre, 1987

I am amused that anyone should think twice at what I think of as my non-face – to be caricatured with wit and affection flatters my ego deliciously!

WENDY HILLER

Driving Miss Daisy, Apollo Theatre, 1988

A simple description of myself would be:
Big nose,
No tits,
Bandy legs.

JANE LAPOTAIRE

Piaf, Royal Shakespeare Company, 1980

> *To A Louse*
> O Wad some Power the giftie gie us
> To see oursels as ithers see us!
> *Burns*
>
> BRIAN COX

Does my face really
resemble a tomahawk?

ANTONY SHER

Richard III, Royal Shakespeare Theatre, Stratford, 1984

King Lear: Howl! Howl! Howl!
LAURENCE OLIVIER

Granada TV, 1983

The day I play the Albert Hall,
gallstones will be jewellery.

MAX WALL

Lizst and I have a lot in common, but...he's been dead *longer* than me.
MAX WALL

As a beauty, I'm not a star;
There are others more handsome by far;
But my face, I don't mind it,
For I am behind it;
It's the people in front get the jar!

ANTHONY QUAYLE

Rehearsing King Lear, 1987

26

I wanted to look the most evil thing there was.
I decided to liberate in every pore of my skin
the utmost libertinism I could imagine.
I stood up, looked in the mirror,
the monster stared back at me – and smiled.

LAURENCE OLIVIER

Richard III, New Theatre, 1949

Acting Shakespeare, the Playhouse Theatre, 198

28

I often feel like this –
I'm only sorry it shows.

IAN McKELLEN

I've so longed to look down my nose
instead of always up it!
But as a character says to Lady Fanciful:
'A little bluntness is a sign of beauty,
which makes me always ready to pardon it.'

DOROTHY TUTIN

The Provok'd Wife, the National Theatre, 1980

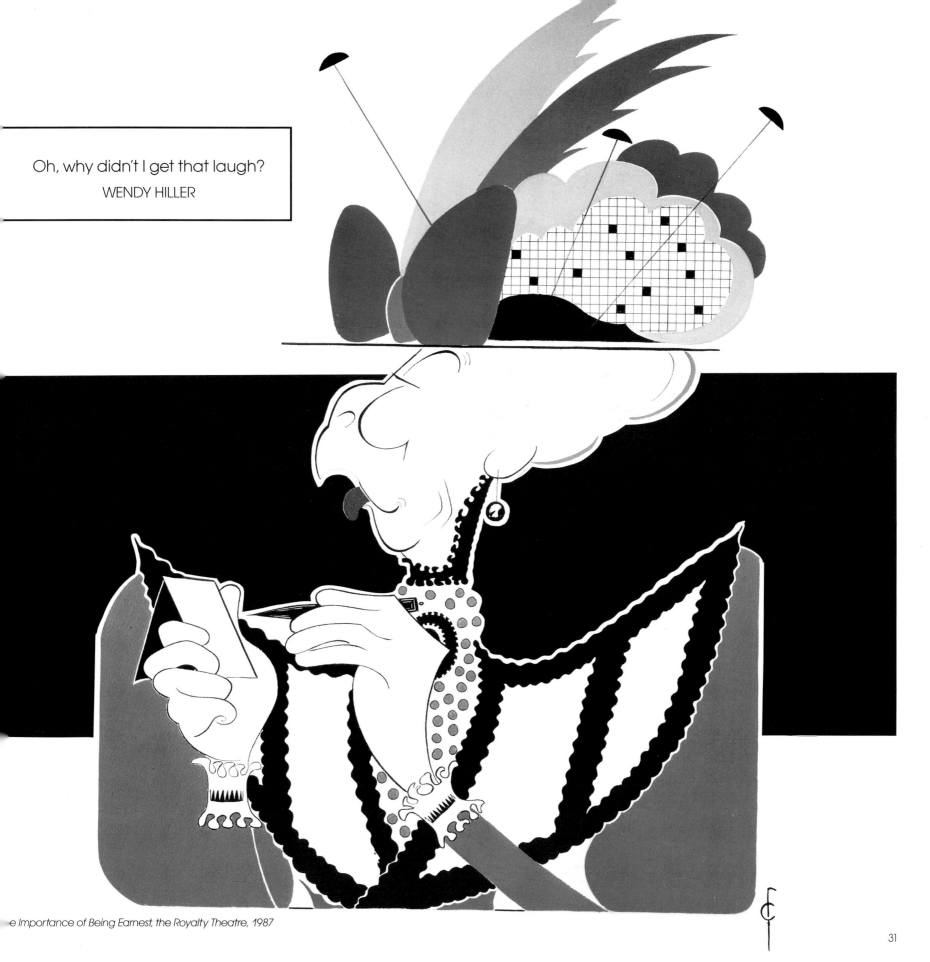

Oh, why didn't I get that laugh?
WENDY HILLER

e Importance of Being Earnest, the Royalty Theatre, 1987

31

Worthing: (aside)
Rather smart
from an Old Bag!

JOHN GIELGUD

The Importance of Being Earnest, the Globe Theatre, 1939/4

The Importance of Being Earnest, the National Theatre, 1982

While we were lurking off-stage
somewhere, knitted up as Goring and Cheveley,
the talk turned to drawing in general
and caricature in particular.
'I suppose,' I said, 'that I would be all
drawing-pin nose and bushy hair?'
And you said, 'No, all teeth and mascara!'

Richard Lester once told me to
keep my mouth shut while we were
filming in the Sahara Desert,
as he was getting a flare off my teeth.
Not unnaturally, I feel as though I am
a paper-shredder crossed with a chipmunk!

JOANNA LUMLEY

An Ideal Husband, Chichester, 1987

'My name is Lettice; as a vegetable
it is obviously one of God's mistakes,
but as a name it passes I think.'

GERALDINE McEWAN

Lettice and Lovage, the Globe Theatre, 1988

ochone

SAMUEL BECKETT

Black – I had to be black.
I had to feel black down to my soul.
If I peeled my skin, underneath would
be another layer of black skin.
I was to be beautiful.
Quite beautiful.

LAURENCE OLIVIER

Othello, the Old Vic, 1964

Seeing a picture of yourself is just as bad
as being unexpectedly ambushed by one's own reflection.
Only worse, because a mirror is a
purely mechanical reproduction of one's feelings,
whereas a portrait includes a human opinion
and that makes the ambush even more dangerous.

JONATHAN MILLER

Oh! God. Have neither of us
got a pair of glasses?

JUDI DENCH AND MICHAEL WILLIAMS

?
MAGGIE SMITH

Lettice and Lovage, the Globe Theatre, 1987

The shoes and the walk helped
me to find the character –
I always start with the feet,
and on this occasion I
finished with the enormous
beauty-spot on Mrs Candor's bust.

BERYL REID

Mountain Language, the National Theatre, 1988

I don't much like my face.
I think it falls somewhere between
Fu Manchu and Desperate Dan –
but a Robert Redford lurks inside.

MICHAEL GAMBON

Tons of Money, the National Theatre, 1986

GWEN FFRANGÇON-DAVIES: *(In her 98th year)*
. . . then, after that there's a Master Class at The National
and another at Stratford, then I'm on 'Wogan'
and then there's 'Desert Island Discs'
and then I've got an interview on LBC
and then there's another Master Class on BBC's Omnibus.

NIGEL HAWTHORNE: *(Somewhat younger!)* Er . . . !

GWEN FFRANGÇON-DAVIES: And after that I'm hoping to write a book
and then, darling, after that there's . . .

NIGEL HAWTHORNE: Good Lord!

Myself as a mess as a mess as Lear!
ANTHONY HOPKINS

The National Theatre, 1987

48

'Chuffed to boogery'...!

EDWARD FOX

Quartermaine's Terms, the Queen's Theatre, 1981

The Entertainer, the Royal Court Theatre, 1957

There he stands in the bright spot-light,
alone, laughless but smiling.
A bowler hat, a cane, eyebrows, a gap
in his teeth and dead eyes.

LAURENCE OLIVIER

Dear Mr Francis, just a line,
(Though all your faces are divine)
How come you catch the others fine
But bring out all the faults in mine?

ALAN AYCKBOURN

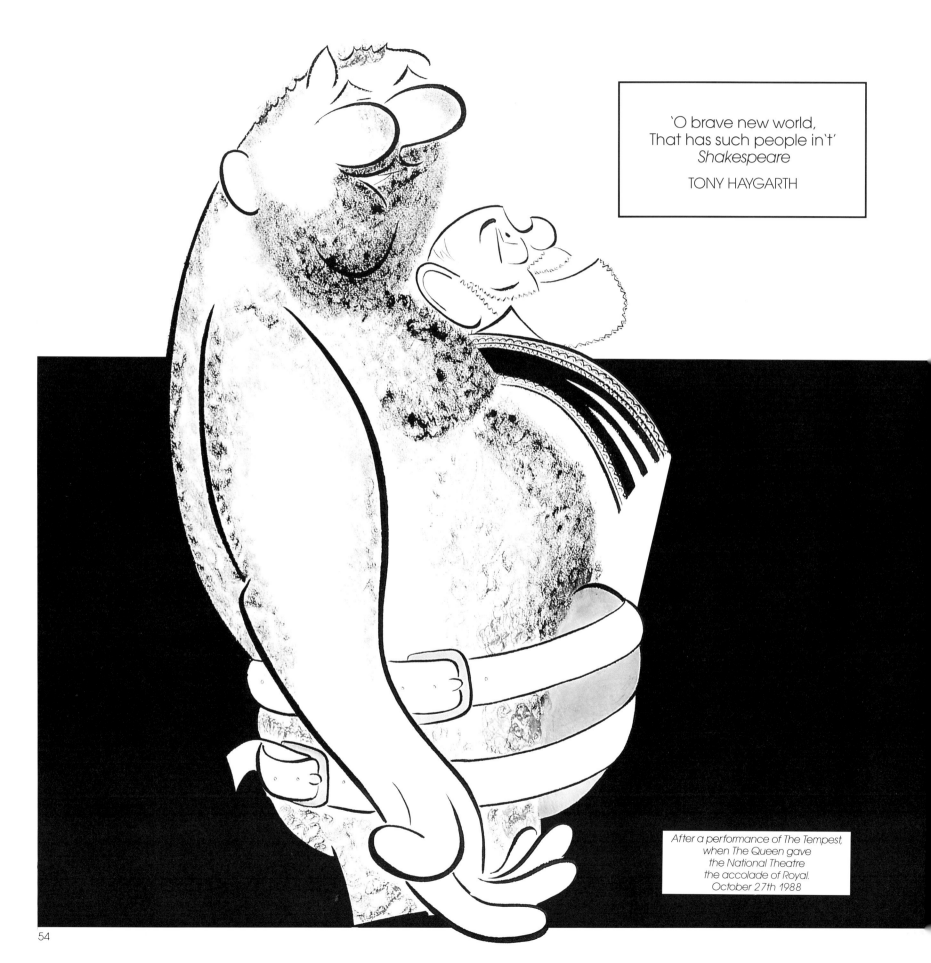

'O brave new world,
That has such people in't'
Shakespeare

TONY HAYGARTH

*After a performance of The Tempest,
when The Queen gave
the National Theatre
the accolade of Royal.
October 27th 1988*

54

No comment.
THE PALACE

55

'Hallo, folks. We're into the Follies.'
DAVID HEALY

The Shaftesbury Theatre, 1987

I look like one of LIBERACE'S bottle openers.

DANIEL MASSEY

Follies, the Shaftesbury Theatre, 1987

Oh, yes, I'm afraid so!
ALEC GUINNESS

59

Only Francis realised it was Jack Lemmon
playing James Tyrone playing Grandma Moses

JACK LEMMON

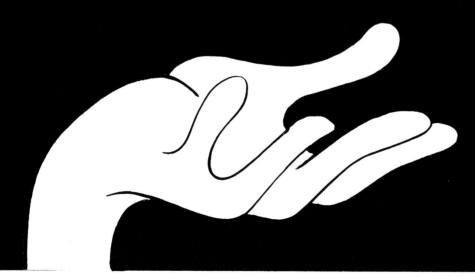

Well I never!
PEGGY ASHCROFT

ANTONY SHER: It's great the way he's made me look like Sylvester Stallone.
ESTELLE KOHLER: Except he's given me the chin!

Hello and Goodbye, the Almeida Theatre, 1988

LAURENCE OLIVIER: . . . !

ALAN BATES: Who did you say this was . . . ?

John Mortimer's A Voyage Round My Father, Thames T.V., 1982

I'm so glad I looked like Alan Bates
when I was young.

JOHN MORTIMER

About this wonderful caricature of my silent play
I have of course, as you see yourself, nothing to say.

MARCEL MARCEAU

I hate the sight
of me either in
the mirror or via
the camera.
So if my face is
a joke I'd sooner
C.F. achieved the laugh!

MICHAEL HORDERN

'The theft of a Pharaoh is something
which hadn't crossed my mind.
Whose mummy is this?' (Loot)

LEONARD ROSSITER as Truscott, Ambassadors Theatre, 1984

Sir RALPH

'I think Auden, don't you?'
I remember saying to Harold Pinter.
'Do you think sandals and socks?'
and he jumped at the idea.
Then I said 'Do you think
we should add spectacles?'
and he liked that too.
About a
week after we started rehearsals
I came on the stage with the wig,
the suit and the spectacles
and everybody said,
'Exactly right, perfect'.
And I said, 'Yes! and now I must
find a performance to go inside it.'

JOHN GIELGUD

Sir JOHN

No Man's Land, the Old Vic, 1975

It was during that week in Edinburgh in 1966,
playing Edgar in *The Dance of Death*, that I
received an exceedingly kind and giddy-making
letter from the Prime Minister, Harold Wilson,
inviting me to accept a peerage.
My immediate reaction was NO, ABSOLUTELY NOT.

A gangling basset-hound,
looking for a comfortable place to rest.

JOHN ALDERTON

Alec McCowen hugging
Stan Laurel,
Max Wall,
Sid Field,
Jack Benny,
Tommy Cooper
and Harpo Marx.

ALEC McCOWEN

Waiting For Godot, the National Theatre, 1988

Can an overcoat be libellous?
Whatever, it still wraps itself
around my lovely young body and
I cannot improve on the long ago
remark that 'it is the sort of
overcoat that Max Miller would
wear to a funeral'.

PETER O'TOOLE

Well, at least I'm smiling!

ARTHUR MILLER

What a pair of thugs.

HAROLD PINTER

Max Harkaway: In the country we rise with the lark.
Sir Harcourt: I haven't the remotest conception when that was!
London Assurance

How brilliantly C.F. has captured
the essence of my delicately under-played
performance in *London Assurance*.

DONALD SINDEN

Royal Shakespeare Compan
Aldwych Theatre, 197

A restless sitter
ALBERT FINNEY

Orphans, the Apollo Theatre, 1986

Guys and Dolls, the National Theatre, 1982

When you're a short, fat,
middle-aged man with a bald head,
any caricature has got to be flattering.

BOB HOSKINS

80

I am so very, very sorry.
STEPHEN FRY

The Common Pursuit, the Phoenix Theatre, 1988

Makes me look suitably spivvy,
which I always feel.

ALAN BENNETT

Since my face has
been compared by critics
with that of a worried hamster,
I think I've been
let off very lightly.

PRUNELLA SCALES

Single Spies, the Queen's Theatre, 1989

My face commonly attracts the adjective 'monkish' but my own favourite description is 'Raymond Huntley... as a boy.'

ALAN BENNETT

That's very good!
A perfect likeness.
TOM STOPPARD

Cheeky!

JULIA McKENZIE

Follies, the Shaftesbury Theatre, 1987

The Phantom of the Opera
ANDREW LLOYD WEBBER

Single Spies, the National Theatre, 1988

The Richard Nixon ski-slope nose,
Frankie Howerd jowls
and a habit, probably subconsciously culled
from the late Margaret Rutherford,
of talking out of the side of my mouth.
I do love the shoes too, which being a clown's
I think actually get to the heart of what I am
always trying to do. I am always trying to find
the clown somewhere behind every character I play;
mainly because I think clowns are essentially
innocent and that's what one wants to celebrate.

SIMON CALLOW

Guy Burgess (*Simon Callow*): My trouble is I lack
what the English call character, by which
they mean the power to refrain.

I used to get a lot of complaints,
culminating in one from a woman who wrote,
'I'm so sorry you used that four-letter word;
it's quite a funny enough play without that.
I have to say,' she added,
'that the man next to me was
lying on the floor barking.'

What the f . . . is going on?
PAUL EDDINGTON

Noises Off, the Savoy Theatre, 1982

Olé!
RICHARD BRIERS

Twelfth Night, Riverside Studios, 1988

How clever to capture, so exactly,
the way I feel first thing in the morning!
ERIC PORTER

Cat on a Hot Tin Roof, the National Theatre, 1

92